WITHOUT A CAUSE

A LOLA COLLECTION

GIRDLE WITHOUT A CAUSE:
A LOLA COLLECTION
2015

PRINTED BY CREATESPACE, AN AMAZON.COM COMPANY
AVAILABLE FROM AMAZON.COM, CREATESPACE.COM, AND
OTHER OUTLETS, INCLUDING

TCTOONZ.COM

ALSO AVAILABLE:
DO-OVERS: A LOLA COLLECTION
LOLA: STRIPS
THE ICE CREAM KID: BRAIN FREEZE!

FOLLOW LOLA ON GOCOMICS.COM OR
WWW.FACEBOOK.COM/LOLACOMIC

LOLA IS SYNDICATED AND DISTRIBUTE
WORLDWIDE BY THE GOOD FOLKS AT
UNIVERSAL UCLICK

ISBN-13: 978-1517718947

TODD CLARK

LOLA

THE ICE CREAM KID

DEDICATED TO:
(YOUR NAME HERE)
MY FAVORITE PERSON
IN THE WORLD!

4

6

9

I CAN'T BELIEVE WHAT AN ODD SONG I'VE GOT STUCK IN MY HEAD.

OOH! IS IT THAT "I'M WALKING ON SUNSHINE, WHOA! AND DON'T IT FEEL GOOD!" SONG?

WELL, IT IS NOW!!

THE LOLA RHYMES

Mary had a little lamb,

whose fleece just wouldn't grow.

Mary found a Rogaine site,

and now it's got a 'fro.

THE LOLA RHYMES

Luke and Lenore went to the store,

to fetch them-selves a soda.

Luke fell down and bonked his crown,

and now he speaks like Yoda.

THE LOLA RHYMES

Mary, Mary ordinary,

how is your garden so pretty?

3/9

With soil and love, and sun from above,

and poop from your dumb neighbor's kitty.

15

18

19

HOW'S SCHOOL, MONTY?

WE'VE BEEN DISCUSSING CAREER OPTIONS.

I TOLD MRS. TRUMBO I WANTED TO BE A TEACHER JUST LIKE HER.

WELL, EXCEPT WITHOUT THE CONTEMPT FOR CHILDREN.

BET THAT WENT OVER WELL.

WHAT'RE YOU WORKNG ON, LOLA?

MY BUCKET LIST.

IS IT PRETTY LENGTHY?

TWO WORDS...

EXTRA CRISPY.

21

26

29

32

I CAUGHT THAT POLITICAL ARGUMENT YOU HAD ON FACEBOOK YESTERDAY.

I MAKE MY CASE WITH SHARP. CLEAR. IRREFUTABLE FACTS.

AND THEN CALL 'IM A DOODYHEAD.

I LIKE A BIG FINISH.

CECIL, WHAT ARE YOU DOING?

GOING TO GET EVIDENCE OF BIGFOOT.

GOT MY CAMPING GEAR, MY MAP OF RECENT SIGHTINGS...

MY CAMERA SET TO "BLUR."

38

40

WOW, LOLA. YOU CAN REALLY SMACK THAT THING.

THE KEY IS TO CHANNEL ALL YOUR ENERGY ON SOME GREAT INJUSTICE. SOMETHING HORRIBLY WRONG IN THE WORLD.

AND WHAT'S THAT FOR YOU?

UNFROSTED POP-TARTS.

THERE'S A BUG IN THIS.

ALL SALES ARE FINAL.

KOOL-AID 50¢

DON'T YOU WANT REPEAT CUSTOMERS?

WHY WOULD I WANT TO HEAR YOU COMPLAIN AGAIN?

TOUCHÉ

EVE BECKER KICKED ME IN THE SHIN.

OUCH.

8/23

SHE'S A GIRL! WHAT CAN I DO IN RETURN?

LET'S SEE, DID YOU CRY OUT IN PAIN?

YEAH.

THEN YOU'RE PRETTY MUCH DONE.

AMY, HAVE YOU SEEN MOM?

SHE WAS GOING TO READ ON THE DECK.

8/24

UH-OH. THAT MEANS DOING BATTLE WITH THE FOLDING LOUNGE CHAIR.

NEED A HAND?

ARE YOU SAYING THERE'S A MORE COMFORTABLE CONFIGURATION?

45

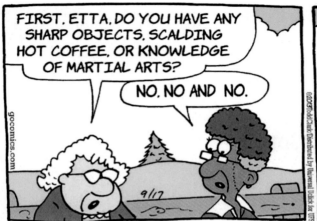

47

49

RAY, I'M GOING TO NEED A DESIGNATED DRIVER.

I THOUGHT YOU WERE GOING BOWLING.

I AM.

THEN WHY WOULD YOU NEED A DESIGNATED DRIVER?

YOUR LACK OF SPORTS KNOWLEDGE IS ASTOUNDING.

GO TO AN ONLINE MED SCHOOL?

ACTUALLY, YES. I DID.

HOW COULD YOU TELL?

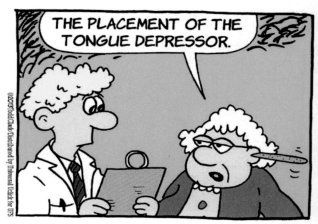

THE PLACEMENT OF THE TONGUE DEPRESSOR.

LOOK WHAT I FOUND IN THE ATTIC.

WHAT IS IT?

IT'S A PHONE, LIKE EVERYONE USED TO HAVE.

WEIRD.

SO, THIS MUST HAVE BEEN THE GIRLS' MODEL?

WHY?

IT'S GOT THIS JUMP ROPE ATTACHED.

RIGHT.

MORNING. AMY. WHAT'S FOR BREAKFAST?

LOLA. I'M UPDATING MY RESUME.

YOU'LL HAVE TO GET IT YOURSELF.

NOW LET'S SEE... SPECIAL SKILLS OR TALENTS?

NEGLECTING SENIORS.

HELPFUL.

54

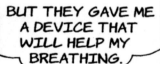

MA'AM, CAN WE COUNT ON A CONTRIBUTION FROM YOU?

WELL...

THINK OF THE CHILDREN, AND THE ELDERLY, AND THE POOR, AND THE SICK, AND THE HUNGRY, AND THE EXTREMELY UGLY, AND...

WHO WAS ON THE PHONE?

NATIONAL GUILT FOUNDATION.

GRANDMA CAN YOU SHOW ME HOW TO TIE A SQUARE KNOT?

I CAN TRY.

YOU WERE IN THE SERVICE. I THOUGHT YOU KNEW THIS STUFF.

THAT'S NAVY.

I WAS ARMY.

YOU GUYS DIDN'T TIE KNOTS?

NO.

WE SHOT AT THE ROPE UNTIL IT COOPERATED.

61

65

BOY, DEAN SURE HAS SELF-ESTEEM ISSUES.

WHY DO YOU THINK THAT?

OH.

I'M WITH STUPID

3/5

RAY, YOU DON'T NEED THE INSTRUCTION MANUAL.

MOTHER...

I'M NOT ONE OF THOSE GUYS. I FIND NOTHING EMASCULATING ABOUT READING THE INSTRUCTIONS.

3/12

STEP ONE: REMOVE OLD BULB FROM SOCKET.

I CAN'T TAKE IT.

GRANDMA RIPPED ONE!

SAMMY!

DON'T BE SO CRUDE.

WHAT? WE WERE FOLDING PAPER AIRPLANES AND SHE RIPPED ONE.

"RIPPED ONE" CAN ALSO MEAN SOMEONE TOOTED.

OH...

IN THAT CASE, SHE RIPPED TWO.

WOW. I GUESS THOSE LITTLE SMART CARS DO SERVE A PURPOSE.

THEY FILL IN THE POTHOLES NICELY.

LOLA

71

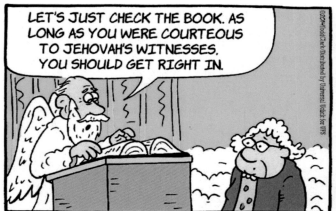

73

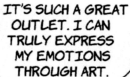

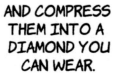

75

76

PASTOR JOHN, ARE LITTLE WHITE LIES PERMISSIBLE?

YOU KNOW, THE KIND WHERE NOBODY REALLY GETS HURT.

IS THIS ABOUT GOLF?

PERHAPS.

MRS. TRUMBO, I'M NOT REALLY FEELING THE WHOLE MATH THING RIGHT NOW.

WELL, MONTY, IT'S EITHER MATH OR HANGING OUT WITH PRINCIPAL THOMPSON.

YOU DON'T SEEM EXCITED ABOUT BEING TODAY'S LUCKY WINNER.

PRINCIPAL

80

WHATCHA WRITING, SAMMY?

A POEM FOR LEEANNE.

AND I MADE IT PERSONAL, LIKE YOU SUGGESTED.

ROSES ARE RED,
YOUR HAIR IS NICE.
MINE'S KINDA DIRTY,
AND LIKELY HAS LICE.

TOO PERSONAL?!

I GOTTA GO BOIL MY HANDS!

BOY, HAVE I HAD A STRING OF BAD LUCK LATELY.

EVERY CLOUD HAS A SILVER LINING.

ZAP!

OR A LIGHTNING BOLT TUCKED BEHIND IT.

83

THANKS FOR LETTING ME PLAY WITH YOU TWO, LOLA.

ABSOLUTELY, PASTOR JOHN.

BEAR IN MIND, I DON'T DRINK, SWEAR OR GAMBLE OUT HERE.

©2014 Todd Clark/Distributed by Universal Uclick for UFS

AND YOU STILL CALL IT GOLF?

SAMUEL, I HOPE TO BE A WRITER SOMEDAY.

UH HUH.

IN ORDER TO DO THAT, I NEED MORE "LIFE EXPERIENCE TO DRAW FROM.

OK.

SO, WE NEED TO BREAK UP, SO I CAN GAIN SOME INSIGHT FROM IT.

LEEANNE, YOU BREAK UP WITH ME ALL THE TIME.

YES, BUT THIS TIME I'VE GOT A REASON.

©2014 Todd Clark/Distributed by Universal Uclick for UFS

HI, SAMMY. HI, MONTY.

HI, MRS. TRUMBO.

BOY, IT'S WEIRD SEEING YOUR TEACHER OUTSIDE OF SCHOOL.

YEAH.

MAKES THEM SEEM ALMOST HUMAN.

WONDER IF THEY KNOW SHE'S ON THE LOOSE?

YES!

WHAT ARE YOU GRINNING ABOUT?

I HIT MY GOAL WEIGHT.

NOW MY GOAL HEIGHT JUST NEEDS TO KICK IN.

87

89

90

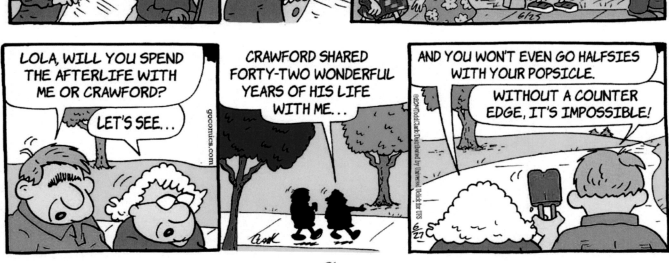

93

94

97

100

104

105

106

WE GATHER TO SAY GOODBYE TO OUR FRIEND, WALTER.

A MAN DEDICATED TO THE ART OF MIME.

NOW TRAPPED IN A BOX FOR ETERNITY.

9/23

SAMUEL, I HAVE A PIANO RECITAL ON SATURDAY.

OK.

9/25

AS MY CURRENT BOYFRIEND, YOUR ATTENDANCE IS MANDATORY.

GOT IT.

AND THE ATTIRE IS FORMAL.

COOL. I CAN BORROW MY GRANDMA'S...

IF YOU SAY TUXEDO T-SHIRT, I'LL WRAP YOUR LIPS AROUND THIS MAILBOX.

MMPHH.

111

112

LEEANNE, I'VE BEEN DOING SOME THINKING.

UH-OH.

AND AS THE MAN IN THIS RELATIONSHIP, I'M GOING TO START CALLING THE SHOTS.

I MEAN, IF THAT'S OK WITH YOU.

I'LL GIVE YOU TUESDAYS FROM 4:00 TO 5:00.

LOLA, YOU HAVE THE FACE OF AN ANGEL.

YOU KNOW...

ASSUMING ANGEL FACES HAVE MUSTARD ON THEM.

YOU NEVER KNOW WHEN TO HIT THE BRAKES, HARRY.

114

THANK YOU

44977923R00066